The Ultimate Book of Random

Fun Facts

By Laadel

Laadel Book

Publishing

Table of contents

Standing around burns calories. On average, a 150 pound person burns 114 calories per hour while standing and doing nothing.

In the original Psycho movie, the blood in the famous shower scene was actually chocolate syrup.

Pope John Paul II was an honorary Harlem Globetrotter.

A crocodile can't move its tongue and cannot chew. Its digestive juices are so strong that it can digest a steel nail.

It snows metal on planet Venus! There are two types that have been found, galena and bismuthinite.

Tom Hanks had an asteroid named after him which was called "12818 tomhanks".

"Strategic incompetence" is the art of avoiding certain tasks by pretending you don't know how to do them.

Humans have been performing dentistry since 7000BC, which makes dentists one of the oldest professions.

Northern Korean people are legally only allowed to have one of 28 haircuts. Men and women can choose from 14 different styles.

The tall chef's hat is called a toque.

Despite Mercury being the closest planet to the Sun, Venus is the warmest planet.

Roughly 33% of cats are not effected by catnip. The euphoric reaction commonly associated with catnip is hereditary.

The Hogwarts Express from the Harry Potter movies is a real train in Scotland.

Being in a negative relationship can weaken your immune system.

Biting someone with false teeth in Louisiana, USA, is considered aggravated assault.

Applying non-fat yogurt to a sunburnt area is a natural way to deal with sunburn.

November 17th is known as "Unfriend Day". On this day you should unfriend anybody who you don't know or speak to.

During World War II, the very first bomb dropped on Berlin by the Allies killed the only elephant in Berlin Zoo.

The smallest thing ever photographed is the shadow of an atom.

Gatorade was invented to help the Florida Gators Football Team stay hydrated.

Greenland voted to leave the European Union in 1985 and have not rejoined since.

Scotland was one of the few countries able to hold off being conquered by the Romans in the first century A.D.

The largest snowflake in the world was found in 1887 it was 15 inches wide and 8 inches thick.

Angelina Jolie performed her own stunts whilst filming Lara Croft: Tomb Raider.

The Latin name for banana is "musa sapientum" which translates to fruit of the wise men.

There is a Guinness world record for the longest amount of time needed to create an official government - it is held by Belgium.

When cellophane was invented in 1908, it was originally intended to be used to protect tablecloths from wine spills.

In the Middle Ages, black pepper was considered a luxury. It was even used to pay rent and taxes on occasion.

Popularized by the Shakespeare play, many people think Julius Caesar's last words were "And you, Brutus?" In reality, he said "You too, my child?"

A standard 12oz jar of honey take 864 bees to produce.

The first Game Boy could run for a staggering 30 hours on only two AA batteries!

The moon was once a piece of the Earth.

Hawaii is the only US state that grows cacao beans to produce chocolate.

Young Tyrannosaurus rex's probably had a thin coat of downy feathers to stay warm. They did not need them as they got older due to their size.

A red blood cell takes only about 20 seconds to make a complete circuit through your body.

Fungus are more closely related to animals on a genetic level than they are to plants.

It is illegal to play a musical instrument in the Northern Territory, Australia, for the purpose of annoying other people.

The Lion King was originally called "King of the Jungle" before they realized that lions don't actually live in jungles.

There is an island called "Just Enough Room", where there's just enough room for a tree and a house.

Every second, the human eye moves about 50 times.

Approximately 1 in every 2,000 babies already has a tooth when they are first born.

I Will Always Love You was originally written and recorded in 1973 by Dolly Parton. It was written as a farewell to her mentor of seven years.

Dogs can be allergic to humans - specifically, their dander. While being treated for this allergy, it can take up to 12 months for a dog to recover.

The average computer user blinks seven times a minute, the normal rate is twenty times per minute.

Credit card EMV chip technology has been around since 1986. It was first implemented in France, with Germany following shortly after.

Deep snow can sometimes appear blue in color because the extra layers of snow create a filter for light.

Most snakes have one lung.

Pearls melt in vinegar.

Of the 70% of water covering the Earth only 3% of it is fresh, the other 97% of it is salted.

The Guinness Book of World Records holds the record for being the book most often stolen from libraries.

The human eye is so sensitive that, if the Earth were flat and it was a dark night, a candle's flame could be seen from 30 miles away.

A giraffe can go longer without water than a camel can.

Rebecca Felton was the first woman to ever serve for the United States Senate - but she only served for one day.

Zebras have only one toe on each foot.

In a human foot there are 26 bones.

Ladybugs bleed from their knees when threatened.

On average, 97 chickens are killed every 0.05 seconds worldwide.

Marie Curie's 100-year-old belongings are still radioactive.

In the United States, each person owns an average of seven pairs of blue jeans. That's one for every day of the week!

Forrest Fenn, an art dealer and author, hid a treasure chest in the Rocky Mountains worth over 1 million dollars. It still has not been found.

Saturn is so big that Earth could fit into it whooping 755 times!

There was once an undersea post office in the Bahamas.

An electric eel can produce a shock of up to 650 volts.

Elephants are the only animals that can't jump.

The pumpkin is a member of the cucurbit family, which are gourds, such as cucumbers and squashes.

A shark is the only animal that can blink both its eyes.

The first meal on the moon was roast turkey, eaten by Niel Armstrong and Buzz Aldrin.

In order to protect themselves from poachers, African Elephants have been evolving without tusks, which unfortunately also hurts their species.

At birth, a baby panda is smaller than a mouse.

The scientific term for brain freeze is "sphenopalatine ganglioneuralgia".

Cruise ships have morgues that can store up to 10 bodies at once. The average amount of people that die on cruise ships per year is 200.

If a frog's mouth is held open for too long the frog will suffocate.

Newborn babies have about 350 bones. They gradually merge and disappear until there are about 206 by the age 5.

The longest unbroken alliance in world history is between England and Portugal. It has lasted since 1386, and still stands today.

Eggs contain most of the recognised vitamins with the exception of vitamin C.

A group of whales is called a pod.

There is an insurance policy issued against alien abduction. Around 50,000 policies have been sold, mainly to residents of the U.S. and England.

The fingerprints of koala bears are virtually indistinguishable from those of humans, so much so that they could be confused at a crime scene.

July 3rd is International Plastic Bag Free Day - it's a day about making a little change to make a big impact (for the better) in the future.

Mosquitoes are attracted to people who just ate bananas.

In Indonesian, there is a word, "Jayus", that means "A joke told so poorly, and so unfunny that one cannot help but laugh".

No one knows just how many stars are in space.

As pure gold is very soft, it is often combined with other things when making jewelry.

The chicken and the ostrich are the closest living relatives of the Tyrannosaurus rex.

Your fingernails grow faster on your dominant hand.

"Death by PowerPoint" is a term relating to the intense boredom of useless PowerPoint presentations.

Snakes and lizards both molt out of their old skin as they grow. Investigators have come to the conclusion that dinosaurs may have also molted.

Reindeer are one of the only mammals that can see UV light.

Americans on average eat 18 acres of pizza in one day.

Venus is the only planet that rotates clockwise.

BTS was the first K-Pop group to get their own Twitter emojis.

Apples, potatoes, and onions all taste the same when eaten with your nose plugged.

It is thought by Russians that eating ice cream will keep you warm.

December 3rd is known as "Roof Over Your Head Day" - a day to be grateful of what we have in life!

The tongue is the only muscle in one's body that is attached from one end.

While watching a Merry-Go-Round from a bench in Griffith Park, Los Angeles, Walt Disney was struck with inspiration for the creation of Disneyland.

McDonald's sells more than 75 burgers per second.

85% of plant life is found in the ocean.

In the 1980's, the founder of Pringles, Fredric Baur, requested to be buried in a Pringles can. His children honored the request.

In "Part 1" of the Battlestar Galactica mini-series, there is a scene where Serenity, the ship from Firefly, can be seen flying through the sky.

Crows can remember the faces of individual humans. They can also hold a grudge.

There are less than 30 ships in the Royal Canadian Navy which is less than most third-world countries.

Without saliva, humans are unable to taste food.

Pure cocoa can help prevent tooth decay. Naturally occurring chemicals in cocoa beans fight harmful bacteria in the mouth.

The word "velociraptor" comes from the Latin words "velox" which means swift, and "raptor" which means robber. Literally - speedy robber!

There's a reply to the saying "Liar, liar, pants on fire" - It's "I don't care, I don't care, I can buy another pair".

The blue whale can produce the loudest sound of any animal. At 188 decibels, the noise can be detected over 800 kilometres away.

Triton, one of Neptune's moons, is gradually getting closer to the planet it orbits.

The oldest webcam stream online today is The San Francisco FogCam, and has been operational since 1994.

Baby owls are called "owlettes"

The average person falls asleep in seven minutes.

The first game to be played in space was Starcraft - Daniel Barry took it with him in 1999 on the Space Shuttle mission STS-96.

In feudal Japan, lords purposely built homes with squeaky floors as a defensive measure against ninjas.

The footprints made on the moon will be there for 100 million years.

Rhubarb can spring up so fast that you can actually hear it grow.

Originally, cigarette filters were made out of cork, the look of which was incorporated into today's pattern.

Albert Einstein had mastered calculus by the tender age of 15.

March 3rd is known as "What if Cats and Dogs Had Opposable Thumbs Day".

79% of pet owners sleep with their pets.

Bill Gates house was designed using a Macintosh Computer.

"Opposites attract" is a common myth. People are actually attracted to people who look like family members, or those with a similar personality type.

A group of horses will not go to sleep at the same time - at least one of them will stay awake to look out for the others.

Mulan has the highest kill-count of any Disney character, including villains, and was the first Disney Princess to be shown killing people on-screen.

The first 4th of July celebration was in 1777.

Starfish don't have brains.

In Kentucky, it is illegal to carry ice-cream in your back pocket.

There are 31,557,600 seconds in a year.

Swedish meatballs originated from a recipe King Charles XII brought back from Turkey in the early 1800s.

There are only two countries in the world that have the color purple in their flags: Nicaragua and Dominica.

Cats which have blue eyes for the duration of their lives are likely to be deaf.

The crocodile is a cannibal; It will occasionally eat other crocodiles.

Iceland has a dating app that stops you hooking up with your cousin.

May 29th is "National Put a Pillow on Your Fridge Day". It is celebrated in Europe & USA to bring luck & wealth to the household.

Mickey Mouse was the first ever cartoon character to talk. In the 1929 episode, The Karnival Kid, Mickey's first words were "Hot dogs!"

The makers of the board game Monopoly print over $50 billion worth of Monopoly money every year.

The process by which bread toasts is called the "Maillard Reaction".

Antimatter is the most expensive substance on earth. It costs roughly $62.5 trillion per gram, or $1.75 quadrillion per ounce.

Ewok Jerky was a popular snack across the Outer Rim in the Star Wars Universe.

Because of its unique tilt, a single night on Uranus lasts for 21 years.

"Dreamt" is the only word in the English language that ends with "mt."

In the 1830s, ketchup was used medicinally.

Queen Elizabeth II is a trained mechanic.

Chewing gum boosts mental proficiency and is considered a better test aid than caffeine - but nobody knows why.

The mongoose is one of those rare animals that is immune to a snake's venom.

The odds of being born on February 29th are 1 in 1461.

Every 10 years, the human skeleton repairs and renews itself. Essentially, you have different bones now than you did 10 years ago!

Tic Tacs got their name from the sound they make when they are tossed around in their container.

The word "oxymoron" is itself an oxymoron. This is because it derives from Ancient Greek where "oxy" means sharp and "moros" means stupid.

There's a city called "Rome" on every continent except Antarctica

Studies found that women have a more heightened sense of smell.

There are presently over a million animal species upon planet earth.

About 25% of all blood from the heart goes into the kidneys.

January 10th is "Peculiar People Day" - a day to celebrate those of us who are a little quirky, weird or eccentric.

In 2007, a 1000-gallon inflatable swimming pool was stolen from someone's back yard without a single drop of water being found!

The human brain is about 75% water.

A bolt of lightning can reach 53,540 degrees Fahrenheit. That's 5 times hotter than the surface of the sun, which is 10,340 degrees Fahrenheit.

It's possible to turn peanut butter into diamonds.

The rhinoceros beetle is the strongest animal and is capable of lifting 850 times its own weight.

The oldest known soup recipe dates back to 6,000 B.C. Among the ingredients? Hippopotamus and sparrow meat.

The thumbs up sign is believed to have originated from Chinese pilots. It was used to communicate with the ground crew before take-off.

Coconut water can be used in an emergency as a substitute for blood plasma.

It takes Uranus 84 years to orbit the Sun once.

Cats have a weak sense of taste they have only 473 taste buds. Humans have 9000.

The Apple Lisa was the first commercial computer with a graphical user interface (GUI) and a mouse.

The "Lost" pilot was so expensive (over $10 million) that the Chairman of ABC was fired for green-lighting the project.

A snail can sleep for 3 years.

There is a geocache on the International Space Station placed in 2008. It has since been visited four times by other astronauts.

Adult cats only meow at humans, not other cats. Kittens meow to their mother but once they get a little older, cats no longer meow to other cats.

Smiling releases endorphins in the body, which makes people feel better.

A study at Florida State University discovered that playing Portal 2 is better for your brain than brain-training games like Lumosity.

Hershey's Kisses are named that after the kissing sound the deposited chocolate makes as it falls from the machine on the conveyor belt.

Chocolate ice cream has been proven to significantly reduce emotional and physical pain.

The world's most remote ATM is run by Wells Fargo in the Antarctic. The ATMs serve around 1,200 residents at the U.S. scientific facility.

There are no turkeys in Turkey.

The voice of Stargazer in Mass Effect 3 was done by Buzz Aldrin.

Suriphobia is the fear of mice.

More than 99.9 percent of all animal species that have ever lived on earth were extinct before the coming of man.

Most catfish are normally active at night, however the Peppered Cory Catfish is active more often during the day.

The highest body count in film history goes to "Lord of the Rings: Return of the King" with 836 on-screen deaths.

The world's smallest mammal, a Bumblebee Bat, weights about the same as a U.S. dime. Native to Myanmar and Thailand, these bats are endangered.

Akon is the #1 selling artist for ringtones in the world.

The first movie ever to put out a motion-picture soundtrack was Snow White and the Seven Dwarves.

Violin bows are commonly made from horse hair.

Junk food is as addictive as drugs.

The British Pound is the world's oldest currency still in use at 1,200 years old. The pound has been an identity as a symbol of British sovereignty.

In Colorado, USA, there is still an active volcano. It last erupted about the same time as the pyramids were being built in Egypt.

When George Washington died, Napoleon Bonaparte of France gave a personal eulogy and ordered a ten day mourning period for France.

Every Pixar movie contains a reference to the Pixar movie that comes after it.

The diameter of Earth is 12,756 km (7,926 miles).

The inventor of Vaseline, Robert Chesebrough, ate a spoonful of the stuff every single day.

Butterflies have their skeletons on the outside of their bodies, this is known as the exoskeleton.

A man who was hanged for his part in the Guy Fawkes Gunpowder Plot had his skin removed and it was used to bind a book that listed his offenses.

John Wilkes Booth's brother once saved the life of Abraham Lincoln's son.

The official beverage of Ohio is tomato juice.

Surgeons who play video games at least 3 hours a week perform 27% faster and make 37% fewer errors.

Gasping for air in a high altitude environment, plus UV light reflecting off snow will cause the roof of your mouth to get sunburnt.

Instead of bones, sharks have a skeleton made from cartilage.

When you have to make a choice, and every choice is a bad one, it's called a zugzwang.

MIT, often cited as one of the world's most prestigious universities, puts almost all of its course materials online for anyone to access for free.

The world's oldest surviving bank is "Banca Monte dei Paschi di Siena", which was founded in 1472, and is currently Italy's 3rd largest bank.

1. What country's entire population was condemned to death by the Spanish inquisition?

2. What are the world's tallest trees?

3. What is the term for an animal or plant that is both male and female?

4. What do tendons join to bones?

5. What country's cavalry used dried milk as long ago as the 13th century?

6. What age preceded the iron age?

7. What author landed a 468 pound marlin without harness in the early 1930's?

8. What credit card features a centurion on its face?

9. What is the great mass of stone trees in the Painted Desert in Arizona called?

10. What does the lacrimal gland produce?

11. What football team was previously known as the Frankford Yellow Jackets?

12. What is the largest country wholly within Europe?

13. What colour is the 'Cookie Monster' from the programme Sesame Street?

14. What does the beast become in beauty & the beast?

15. What flightless bird became extinct in 1681 after being devoured by Europeans for food?

16. What do the seven stripes on the American flag represent?

17. What is the name of the cartilage flap at the trachea which prevents food going down the wrong way?

18. What capital city overlooks the River Tagus?

19. What is the more common name for 'self contained underwater breathing apparatus?

20. What did American Harland D. Sanders give to the world in 1939?

21. What Georgia park features carvings on the world's largest piece of exposed granite?

22. What is the game we call Noughts and Crosses called in America?

23. Name the character played by Frank Sinatra in films such as Lady in Cement?

24. What is the title of John Lennon's first published book?

25. What country played West Germany in soccers world cup finals in both 1986 & 1990?

26. What colour is the Ferrari emblem?

27. What is the name used to describe materials that can be broken down by nature?

28. What is a boats speed measured in?

29. What is the term for precipitation that has been polluted by sulfur dioxide & nitrogen oxides?

30. What fruit were the golden apples of greek mythology?

31. What do you call a large linear molecule that is formed from many simple molecules?

32. What ability has the silkworm moth lost through domestication?

33. What did the Celts consider sacred because it communicated moisture from the ground into the air?

34. What is the white semicircle on a fingernail?

35. What branch of science studies the motion of air & the forces acting on objects in air?

36. What is the name of the ridge seperating two glacial valleys?

37. What is the term used by the military when they lose a nuclear weapon?

38. What is the spiral galaxy nearest ours?

39. What drink is a mixture of white wine and blackcurrant syrup or liqueur?

40. How many 'tarsal' bones do we have in each foot?

41. What does a cat use to determine if a space is too small to squeeze through?

42. What bird lays an egg the size of a pea?

43. What is the name of the Chicago baseball team based at Wrigley Field?

44. What 2 countries border the Dead Sea?

45. What do you call marine echinoderms having 5 arms extending from a central disc?

46. What is the Mexican dish 'huevos rancheros' made from?

47. What do we call in English the type of painting known to the French as 'nature morte'?

48. What became the biggest use for aluminum starting in 1960?

49. What famous gift did King Arthur receive when he wed Queen Guinevere?

50. What city is also known as Beantown?

51. How did loggers get their logs to the mills in the 18th & 19th century?

52. What is the deepest lake in the world?

53. How long can it take for the insecticide DDT to break down in nature?

54. What colour comes between yellow & blue in a rainbow?

55. What did Atlanta pharmacist John Pemberton sell two-thirds of his interest in for 283 dollars and 29 cents in 1887?

56. What is the most reliable geyser in the world?

57. What Edwin Budding invention began changing the face of English landscapes in the 1820s?

58. What is the common name for the 'pharynx'?

59. What is the name of the CIA agent played by Harrison Ford in Patriot Games and Clear and Present Danger?

60. What is the name of Morticia's husband in TV's 'Addams Family'?

61. What in Paris was erected to celebrate the anniversary of the French revolution?

62. What is a very thin pastry used in Mediterranean cooking?

63. What does a soccer player have to do when the referee shows him a red card?

64. What causes baker's itch?

65. What did the 1980 U S naval academy class have for the first time in history?

66. What does a la carte mean in a restaurant?

67. What is the alternative name of Beethoven's sonata number 14 in C sharp minor?

68. What country's currency features a portrait of John Tebbutt?

69. What are the sandals called that are worn in ceremonial japanese tradition?

70. What is SAD?

71. Name the North African spicy dish of steamed semolina served with meat stew?

72. What country did Siam become?

73. What do you call substances that will not let thermal heat pass through them?

74. What is the name of the oath which doctor's must take?

75. Waves break when their height is how much more than the depth of the water?

76. What country did Christopher Columbus insist Cuba was a part of?

77. Nancy Cartwright and Yeardley Smith provide the voices for which brother and sister on television?

78. What does an oologist study?

79. What 1982 horror film starred JoBeth Williams as a woman whose youngest child is carried off into a TV set?

80. What is a group of geese called?

81. How many watches are there in the course of a sailor's day (24 hours)?

82. What European country administers the island of Martinique?

83. What did the Romans call the tenth part of a legion - between 300 and 600 men?

84. What famous painting was also known as la Gioconda?

85. What famous geyser erupts regularly at the Yellowstone National Park?

86. What is the literal translation of the word brandy?

87. Name the legendary Hollywood cowboy who was born as Leonard Slye in 1912?

88. What does an insect do when it moults?

89. What is a vein or fissure in a rock containing mineral deposits called?

90. What are the membranes enveloping the brain and spinal cord called?

91. What is the term of an animal with pure white skin & hair & pink eyes?

92. What instrument on a car measures distance?

93. What do Indianapolis 500 winners traditionally drink in the winners circle?

94. What animals give birth to fawns?

95. What compound is often added to water supplies to help prevent toth decay?

96. What are loose rocks on a mountainside called?

97. What ailing founding father was carted to the Constitutional Convention in a sedan chair carried by four prisoners?

98. What are you doing if you are ledgering?

99. What is the name of the cold Spanish soup made from peppers and tomatoes?

100. What are lime deposits growing up from the floor of a cave called?

101. What is the name of the weak attractive bonds which exist between molecules?

102. What do x & y chromozomes combine in making?

103. How many pieces are on the board at the start of a game of backgammon?

104. How long is a standard Olympic swimming pool?

105. What blonde was the subject of the four most expensive Andy Warhol works sold at auction?

106. What is Ronald Reagan's middle name?

107. Name the French blue-veined cheese that is ripened in limestone caves?

108. What branch of biology concentrates on heredity?

109. What alternative name is given to the Barn Owl because of its harsh cry?

110. What date is the 'Ides' of March?

111. What is the name of an animal that can pass on bacteria without being affected by the disease itself?

112. What color are an albino elephant's toenails?

113. What is the name given to the side opposite the right angle of a right-angled triangle?

114. What are the siberian prison islands also known as?

115. How many singles titles did Martina Navratilova pick up at Wimbledon?

116. What declaration warned against interference in the America's?

117. What is the name of the tube connecting the middle ear with the pharynx?

118. What instrument is used to measure atmospheric pressure?

119. What is the unit of measurement which is equal to the mean distance from the Earth to the Sun?

120. What continent is home to half the worlds people?

121. What character was invented to respond to questions from Gold Medal Flour customers?

122. What in Dickensian London was the Marshalsea?

123. What is the anatomical name for the bones of a human's fingers and toes?

124. What is a mayonnaise flavoured with garlic called?

125. How many continents must a sport be regularly played in before it is accepted into the olympics?

126. What bird makes an excellent watchdog?

127. What character did Michael J Fox play in the film Back to the Future?

128. What are the dots called on dominoes?

129. What astronomical unit of distance is used for measurements beyond the solar system?

130. What is a naevus (nevus)?

131. What is the traditional theatrical greeting before a performance to wish 'good luck'?

132. What is the latin name for modern man?

133. What celebrated photographer snapped shots of Yosemite for 67 straight years?

134. What do you get by mixing gin & vermouth?

135. What is the largest lizard on earth at ten feet long & up to 250 pounds?

136. How many cars compete against each other in a drag race?

137. What is the title of the sequel to the book Gentlemen Prefer Blondes by Anita Loos?

138. What is a pugilist?

139. What Ernest Hemingway novel depicts the lives of rebels during the Spanish civil war?

140. What force is the opposite of centripetal force?

141. What is the medical term given to the study of the brain and nervous system?

142. What automaker bought Rolls Royce in 1998?

143. Name the computer which beat World Chess Champion Garry Kasparov in 1997?

144. What animal helped free the trapped lion in Aesop's fable?

145. What is the term for a small umbrella used to protect a person from the sun?

146. What does the Greek word eureka mean?

147. What breed of sheepdog was developed in Australia from Scottish collies?

148. How many spikes do the shoes of a hammer thrower have?

149. What canal parts redesigned by Leonardo da Vinci in 1497 are still in use today?

150. What color is produced by the complete absorption of light rays?

151. What are the lime deposits hanging from the ceiling of a cave called?

152. What country's been the site of the most European battles?

153. What city's underground railroad system has the most stations (458) of any in the world?

154. What does 'rio de janeiro' mean in portuguese?

155. What college handbook edited by Lisa Birnbach described how to be really top drawer?

156. What drug is obtained from the leaves of the coca plant?

157. What famous thinker proved a lunar eclipse is the circular shadow of the earth on the moon?

158. What is the more common name of nitrous oxide?

159. What is the name of the high quality parchment made on a basis of goat or calf skin?

160. Name the only country with a national dog?

161. What did the repair technicians of the first 'modern' computers wear while working?

162. What are looser than normal in a double jointed person?

163. What does the Fleetwood Mac inspired plaque on Bill Clinton's desk read?

164. What is the middle name of author H.G. Wells?

165. What is the largest volcano in our solar system & what planet is it on?

166. What is the former name of Istanbul?

167. Name the character played by David Cassidy in television's Partridge Family series of the 1970s?

168. What does a petrologist study?

169. What is the name of the fibrous protein present in the outer layer of the skin and in hair and nails?

170. What is the middle name of author Arthur C. Clarke?

171. What Canadian province was the site of England's first overseas possession?

172. What berries give gin its flavour?

173. What is the name given to the young of 'dragonflies' and 'damselflies'?

174. What are the two main islands of the Philippines?

175. What is the term for the period of change in form of an organism from the larval to the adult stage?

176. What is the national flower of Scotland?

177. What ancient measure was the distance from the elbow to the tip of the middle finger?

178. Name the painting medium which involves the use of egg yolks?

179. What are the only two London boroughs that start with the letter 'e'?

180. What does the king of spades hold in his left hand?

181. What is the name of the steam train which gained the world speed record in 1938?

182. What animals became the leaders in Animal Farm?

183. What is the name of the big muscle used in breathing that seperates the chest from the abdomen?

184. What citrus fruit shares it's name with a major Chinese language?

185. What does one call the two areas on either side of the seine river in France?

186. What flower asks not to be forgotten?

187. What is the name of the water-soluble simple sugar found in both honey and fruit?

188. What continent did Britain first begin to colonise in 1788?

189. What is the mathematical diagram in which sets are represented by overlapping circles?

190. What animal's hair is used in violin bows?

191. Name the first ship from which Gulliver was shipwrecked in 'Gulliver's Travels'?

192. What are the male organs of a flower called?

193. What do we call the noise made by a sudden spasm closing the windpipe?

194. What country's people were taxed for using salt in the 17th century?

195. What has accumulated in the muscles in someone suffering from emphysema?

196. What is another name for the Yeti?

197. What city boasts a World of Coca Cola pavillion featuring futuristic soda fountains?

198. How many musicians are there in a nonet?

199. What is the Chinese practice of treating illness by inserting needles into the body called?

200. What do Americans call 'candy floss'?

1. Who did Aaron Burr kill?

    A. Abraham Lincoln

    B. Alexander Hamilton

    C. George Washington

    D. Thomas Jefferson

2. What American beer has been long promoted as the King of Beers?

    A. Budweiser

    B. Heineken

    C. Bud Light

    D. PBR

3. Which country has cross country skiing as its national sport?

    A. Japan

    B. USA

    C. Norway

    D. Switzerland

4. How many legs does a lobster have?

    A. 6

    B. 8

    C. 10

    D. 12

5. What profession did Spartacus have?

    A. Politician

    B. Slave

    C. Gladiator

    D. Farmer

6. What was the first mammal to be sent into space?

    A. dog

    B. guinea pig

    C. monkey

    D. mouse

7. The Forbidden City is located in which country?

    A. China

    B. Angola

    C. Uganda

    D. Mexico

8. How many countries are part of Great Britain?

    A. 3

    B. 4

    C. 5

    D. 2

9. In which city did Anne Frank hide from the Nazis?

    A. Berlin

    B. Paris

    C. Warsaw

    D. Amsterdam

10. What was the ice cream cone invented for?

    A. To hold pens

    B. To use in bowling

    C. To hold flowers

    D. To eat by itself

11. What is the most linguistically diverse country in the world?

    A. Papua New Guinea

    B. USA

    C. Australia

    D. Ireland

12. Which among these countries was NOT part of the World War I?

    A. Switzerland

    B. Germany

    C. France

    D. Japan

13. Distance is equal to speed multiplied by what?

    A. acceleration

    B. length

    C. time

    D. velocity

14. What country produced the most strawberries in 2016?

    A. USA

    B. Mexico

    C. Brazil

    D. China

15. Shintoism originated from which country?

    A. India

    B. South Korea

    C. Japan

    D. Thailand

16. What character did Michael J. Fox play in Back to the Future?

    A. London McFly

    B. Marty McFly

    C. George McFly

    D. Dave McFly

17. In which country is the Troi-Rivieres bridge?

A. France

B. Canada

C. Vietnam

D. Algeria

18. Which river flows through Paris?

A. River Seine

B. Moon River

C. River Thames

D. Yellow River

19. What was branch of science was Ernest Rutherford famous for?

A. botany

B. meteorology

C. paleontology

D. radioactivity

20. What was the name of the first satellite launched into space?

A. Atlas

B. Apollo I

C. Mir

D. Sputnik I

21. Who was the first pope of Rome?

   A. Paul
   B. John
   C. Peter
   D. Adam

22. Ludwig Van Beethoven was born in 1770 in which city?

   A. Berlin
   B. Vienna
   C. Prague
   D. Munich

23. Which of these is not a type of quark?

   A. charm
   B. down
   C. round
   D. up

24. Which civilization invented the wheel?

   A. Egypt
   B. China
   C. Rome
   D. Mesopotamia

25. Florence Nightingale aided the sick and wounded during what war?

    A. The Boer Wars
    B. The War of 1812
    C. The Crimean War
    D. The Revolutionary War

26. Which gas makes up 91% of the sun?

    A. helium
    B. hydrogen
    C. nitrogen
    D. oxygen

27. What is the largest type of deer?

    A. Bull
    B. Moose
    C. Stag
    D. Big Antler

28. How many teeth does an aardvark have?

    A. 12
    B. 32
    C. 2
    D. None

29. Who proposed the Big Bang theory of the universe in 1927?

A. Nicholas Copernicus

B. Galileo Galilei

C. Stephen Hawking

D. George Lemaître

30. It is illegal to do what in the French vineyards?

A. Have a picnic

B. Curse

C. Die

D. Land a flying saucer

31. Yao Ming played for this NBA team:

A. Houston Rockets

B. Golden State Warriors

C. New Orleans Pelicans

D. Atlanta Hawks

32. How many hearts does an octopus have?

A. 1

B. 3

C. 4

D. 8

33. According to Greek myth who had snakes for hair?

    A. Medusa

    B. Venus

    C. Artemia

    D. Aphrodite

34. Which of these animals is most harmful to humans?

    A. basking shark

    B. hippopotamus

    C. manta ray

    D. vampire bat

35. Which of these animals would not be found in the arctic circle?

    A. arctic fox

    B. penguin

    C. polar bear

    D. walrus

36. Who was the last tsar of Russia?

    A. Nicholas II

    B. Alexander II

    C. Paul I

    D. Catherine II

37. What was the Titanic's official job?

    A. Deliver mail

    B. passenger liner

    C. cargo ship

    D. carry animals

38. Where is the Machu Picchu located?

    A. Nepal

    B. Brazil

    C. Peru

    D. Myanmar

39. Who designed the current U.S flag?

    A. Robert Borden

    B. Robert Heft

    C. Daniel Peterson

    D. Bill Young

40. An ohm is a measure of what?

    A. current

    B. power

    C. resistance

    D. voltage

41. Where was the world's smallest fish discovered?

    A. Indonesia

    B. Brazil

    C. Australia

    D. Turkey

42. What does a Scoville unit measure?

    A. Acidity

    B. Aroma

    C. Spiciness

    D. Heat

43. Why are hockey pucks frozen before a game?

    A. To prevent their breaking up

    B. To prevent them from bouncing

    C. To add strength

    D. To prevent injuries to players

44. The mountain bongo is native to which country?

    A. Australia

    B. Kenya

    C. Turkey

    D. Nepal

45. What did Philip II of Macedon lose during battle?

A. Teeth

B. finger

C. ear

D. eye

46. When did the Cold War end?

A. 1978

B. 1989

C. 1991

D. 1994

47. Which country has the most number of UNESCO Heritage Sites?

A. India

B. Italy

C. England

D. Germany

48. Which country has the most mountains?

A. India

B. USA

C. China

D. Russia

49. Who started the Russian Revolution?

    A. Joseph Stalin
    B. Vladimir Lenin
    C. Sergei Witte
    D. Peter Stolypin

50. Which of these is not a method of heat transfer?

    A. conduction
    B. convection
    C. evaporation
    D. radiation

51. How much DNA do humans share with bananas?

    A. 0%
    B. 5%
    C. 50%
    D. 90%

52. Which is the main substance used to make a crayon?

    A. Dye
    B. Wax
    C. Plastic
    D. Chalk

53. What is the ancient name of Taiwan?

A. Formosa

B. Taipei

C. Peking

D. Hanoi

54. Which below sea level mountain is taller than Mt. Everest?

A. Mauna Kea

B. Mount Vema

C. Maud Seamount

D. Belgica Guyot

55. Which author wrote the Winnie-the-Pooh books?

A. Dr, Seuss

B. Roald Dahl

C. A. A. Milne

D. Beatrix Potter

56. What kind of an animal is known as a horned toad?

A. A frog

B. A lizard

C. A beetle

D. A toad

57. What is the largest lizard?

    A. Gila

    B. Water dragon

    C. Komodo dragon

    D. Alligator

58. What is Bob Dylan's real name?

    A. Lind Zimmerman

    B. Robert Zimmerman

    C. Adam Zimmerman

    D. Jonathan Zimmerman

59. In the game of pool what is the standard color for the one ball?

    A. Blue

    B. Red

    C. Yellow

    D. Green

60. What was Toyota's first popular hybrid car called?

    A. Yaris

    B. Matrix

    C. Prius

    D. Camry

61. Which among these countries is still led by a monarch?

    A. Saudi Arabia
    B. Egypt
    C. Portugal
    D. France

62. Which country is known as the Land of White Elephant?

    A. India
    B. Thailand
    C. Cambodia
    D. Vietnam

63. Who wrote Around the World in 80 Days?

    A. Jules Verne
    B. Herman Melville
    C. Tom Clancy
    D. Bram Stoker

64. Where did rap superstar Eminem grow up?

    A. Detroit
    B. Chicago
    C. St. Louis
    D. Los Angeles

65. Who invented scissors?

    A. Hero of Alexander

    B. Leonardo da Vinci

    C. Johannes Guttenberg

    D. Hans Janssen

66. Which country owns the Galapagos Islands?

    A. Spain

    B. Ecuador

    C. Papua New Guinea

    D. Portugal

67. What number did Derek Jeter wear on his New York Yankees jersey?

    A. 4

    B. 11

    C. 2

    D. 7

68. A puffball is a type of what?

    A. fish

    B. frog

    C. fungi

    D. parrot

69. Copper and tin can be combined to make which metal alloy?

A. brass

B. bronze

C. gold

D. pewter

70. What does the word Matrix mean in the Bible?

A. Womb

B. Burial place

C. Heaven

D. Prophet

71. Dutch people live in which country?

A. Georgia

B. Netherlands

C. Belgium

D. Denmark

72. Where do the Grimm's fairy tales originate from?

A. Germany

B. France

C. Russia

D. Netherlands

73. What country won the very first FIFA World Cup in 1930?

A. Uruguay

B. Italy

C. Brazil

D. England

74. Which of the following energy sources is non-renewable?

A. fossil fuels

B. hydroelectric

C. solar power

D. wind power

75. Which of these elements is not a metal?

A. mercury

B. neon

C. sodium

D. tungsten

76. What is the rarest M&M color?

A. Yellow

B. Green

C. Brown

D. Blue

77. What is the name of Jordan's capital city?

A. Amman

B. Damascus

C. Jericho

D. Shiraz

78. Which Roman Emperor liked to fight in games?

A. Commodus

B. Trajan

C. Titus

D. Caligula

79. Who discovered King Tut's tomb?

A. Henry Wilson

B. Howard Carter

C. Charles Smith

D. Edward Peters

80. Which country was the first to use paper currency?

A. England

B. France

C. China

D. India

81. Where was the U.S. largest surrender in battle?

    A. Bataan
    B. Berlin
    C. Paris
    D. Tokyo

82. What is the family name of the ruling dynasty of Monaco?

    A. Gorgio
    B. Giovanni
    C. Grimidi
    D. Grimaldi

83. What grows from an acorn?

    A. Oak Tree
    B. Maple Tree
    C. Birch Tree
    D. Pine Tree

84. When a people are frightened their ears produce more of what?

    A. Earwax
    B. Sweat
    C. Ringing sounds
    D. White blood cells

85. In 1917 Finland declared its independence from which country?

A. Sweden

B. Norway

C. Denmark

D. Russia

86. Which continent is in all four hemispheres?

A. Africa

B. Asia

C. Antarctica

D. Europe

87. Who was said to float like a butterfly and sting like a bee??

A. The Dalai Lama

B. Muhammed Ali

C. Buddha

D. Sun Tzu

88. What is the world's most venomous fish?

A. Stingray

B. Stonefish

C. Shark

D. Pufferfish

89. What christian denomination was founded by John Wesley in 1738?

    A. Methodist
    B. Anabaptist
    C. Episcopalianism
    D. Pentecostal

90. The longest bridge in the world is located in which country

    A. China
    B. USA
    C. Russia
    D. Ecuador

91. Who introduced the world's first mass-produced car?

    A. Louis Chevrolet
    B. Walter Chrysler
    C. Henry Ford
    D. William Durant

92. Which country was Joseph Stalin born in?

    A. Georgia
    B. Ukraine
    C. Russia
    D. Serbia

93. What is the longest river?

   A. Yellow River
   B. Congo River
   C. Nile
   D. Mekong River

94. In which U.S. state was the atomic bomb tested in?

   A. New York
   B. New Mexico
   C. Nevada
   D. Texas

95. How many US states begin with the letter A?

   A. 4
   B. 5
   C. 8
   D. 2

96. The southern tip of South America has what name?

   A. Cape Horn
   B. Cape Town
   C. Ushuaia
   D. Buenos Aires

97. Who wrote Frankenstein?

    A. Mary Shelley

    B. Percy Shelley

    C. Franklin Stein

    D. Howard Young

98. Which of these instruments is used to measure wind speed?

    A. anemometer

    B. barometer

    C. hygrometer

    D. wind vane

99. How many U.S. Presidents were named James?

    A. 3

    B. 6

    C. 7

    D. 1

100. King Henry VI of England was also the king of which country?

    A. Spain

    B. Italy

    C. France

    D. Russia

1. Netherlands

2. Coast Redwoods

3. Hermaphrodite

4. Muscles

5. Mongolia

6. Bronze Age

7. Ernest Hemingway

8. American Express

9. The Petrified Forest

10. Tears

11. Philadelphia Eagles

12. France

13. Blue

14. A Prince

15. Dodo Bird

16. The Seven Original States

17. Epiglottis

18. Lisbon

19. Scuba

20. Kentucky Fried Chicken

21. Stone Mountain

22. Tic Tac Toe

23. Tony Rome

24. In His Own Write

25. Argentina

26. Yellow

27. Biogradable

28. Knots

29. Acid Rain

30. Apricots

31. Polymer

32. Flight

33. Trees

34. Lunula

35. Aerodynamics

36. Arete

37. Broken Arrow

38. Andromeda

39. Kir

40. Seven

41. Whiskers

42. Hummingbird

43. Chicago Cubs

44. Israel And Jordan

45. Shekel

46. Baked Eggs

47. Still Life

48. Tin Cans

49. Round Table

50. Boston

51. Floated Down Rivers

52. Lake Baikal

53. Eight Years

54. Green

55. Coca Cola

56. Old Faithful

73. Insulators

74. Hippocratic

75. Seven Tenths

76. China

77. Bart & Lisa Simpson

78. Bird's Eggs

79. Poltergeist

80. Gaggle

81. Six

82. France

83. A Cohort

84. Mona Lisa

85. Old Faithful

86. Burnt Wine

87. Roy Rogers

88. Sheds Its Skin

89. Lode

90. Meninges

91. Albino

92. Odometer

93. Milk

94. Deer

95. Fluoride

96. Scree

97. Benjamin Franklin

98. Fishing

99. Gazpacho

100. Stalacmites

101. Van Der Waals Forces

102. Males

103. Thirty

104. Fifty Metres

105. Marilyn Monroe

106. Wilson

107. Roquefort

108. Genetics

109. Screech Owl

110. Fifteenth

111. Vector

112. White

113. Hypoteneuse

114. Gulag Archipelego

115. Nine

116. Monroe Doctrine

117. Eustachian Tube

118. Barometer

119. Astronomical Unit

120. Asia

121. Betty Crocker

122. Debtors Prison

123. Phalanges

124. Aioli

125. Five

126. Goose

127. Marty Mcfly

128. Pips

129. Parsec

130. Birthmark

131. Break A Leg

132. Homo Sapiens

133. Ansel Adams

134. Martini

135. Komodo Dragon

136. Two

145. Parasol

146. I Have Found It

147. Kelpie

148. None

149. Locks

150. Black

151. Stalactites

152. Belgium

169. Keratin

170. Charles

171. Newfoundland

172. Juniper Berries

173. Nymphs

174. Mindanao & Luzon

175. Metamorphosis

176. Thistle

177. Cubit

178. Tempera

179. Ealing & Enfield

180. Sword

181. Mallard

182. Pigs

183. Diaphragm

184. Mandarin

193. Hiccup

194. France

195. Air

196. Abominable Snowman

197. Atlanta

198. Nine

199. Acupuncture

200. Cotton Candy

1. Who did Aaron Burr kill?

   Alexander Hamilton

2. What American beer has been long promoted as the King of Beers?

   Budweiser

3. Which country has cross country skiing as its national sport?

   Norway

4. How many legs does a lobster have?

   10

5. What profession did Spartacus have?

   Gladiator

6. What was the first mammal to be sent into space?

   Monkey

7. The Forbidden City is located in which country?

   China

8. How many countries are part of Great Britain?

   3

9. In which city did Anne Frank hide from the Nazis?

Amsterdam

10. What was the ice cream cone invented for?

To hold flowers

11. What is the most linguistically diverse country in the world?

Papua New Guinea

12. Which among these countries was NOT part of the World War I?

Switzerland

13. Distance is equal to speed multiplied by what?

Time

14. What country produced the most strawberries in 2016?

China

15. Shintoism originated from which country?

Japan

16. What character did Michael J. Fox play in Back to the Future?

Marty McFly

17. In which country is the Troi-Rivieres bridge?

Canada

18. Which river flows through Paris?

River Seine

19. What was branch of science was Ernest Rutherford famous for?

Radioactivity

20. What was the name of the first satellite launched into space?

Sputnik I

21. Who was the first pope of Rome?

Peter

22. Ludwig Van Beethoven was born in 1770 in which city?

Berlin

23. Which of these is not a type of quark?

Round

24. Which civilization invented the wheel?

Mesopotamia

25. Florence Nightingale aided the sick and wounded during what war?

The Crimean War

26. Which gas makes up 91% of the sun?

Hydrogen

27. What is the largest type of deer?

Moose

28. How many teeth does an aardvark have?

None

29. Who proposed the Big Bang theory of the universe in 1927?

George Lemaître

30. It is illegal to do what in the French vineyards?

Land a flying saucer

31. Yao Ming played for this NBA team:

Houston Rockets

32. How many hearts does an octopus have?

3

33. According to Greek myth who had snakes for hair?

Medusa

34. Which of these animals is most harmful to humans?

Hippopotamus

35. Which of these animals would not be found in the arctic circle?

Penguin

36. Who was the last tsar of Russia?

Nicholas II

37. What was the Titanic's official job?

deliver mail

38. Where is the Machu Picchu located?

Peru

39. Who designed the current U.S flag?

Robert Heft

40. An ohm is a measure of what?

Resistance

41. Where was the world's smallest fish discovered?

Indonesia

42. What does a Scoville unit measure?

Spiciness

43. Why are hockey pucks frozen before a game?

To prevent them from bouncing

44. The mountain bongo is native to which country?

Kenya

45. What did Philip II of Macedon lose during battle?

eye

46. When did the Cold War end?

1989

47. Which country has the most number of UNESCO Heritage Sites?

Italy

48. Which country has the most mountains?

USA

49. Who started the Russian Revolution?

   Vladimir Lenin

50. Which of these is not a method of heat transfer?

   Evaporation

51. How much DNA do humans share with bananas?

   50%

52. Which is the main substance used to make a crayon?

   Wax

53. What is the ancient name of Taiwan?

   Formosa

54. Which below sea level mountain is taller than Mt. Everest?

   Mauna Kea

55. Which author wrote the Winnie-the-Pooh books?

   A. A. Milne

56. What kind of an animal is known as a horned toad?

   A lizard

57. What is the largest lizard?

   Komodo dragon

58. What is Bob Dylan's real name?

   Robert Zimmerman

59. In the game of pool what is the standard color for the one ball?

   Yellow

60. What was Toyota's first popular hybrid car called?

   Prius

61. Which among these countries is still led by a monarch?

   Saudi Arabia

62. Which country is known as the Land of White Elephant?

   Thailand

63. Who wrote Around the World in 80 Days?

   Jules Verne

64. Where did rap superstar Eminem grow up?

   Detroit

65. Who invented scissors?

Leonardo da Vinci

66. Which country owns the Galapagos Islands?

Ecuador

67. What number did Derek Jeter wear on his New York Yankees jersey?

2

68. A puffball is a type of what?

Fungi

69. Copper and tin can be combined to make which metal alloy?

Bronze

70. What does the word Matrix mean in the Bible?

Womb

71. Dutch people live in which country?

Netherlands

72. Where do the Grimm's fairy tales originate from?

Germany

73. What country won the very first FIFA World Cup in 1930?

Uruguay

74. Which of the following energy sources is non-renewable?

Fossil fuels

75. Which of these elements is not a metal?

Neon

76. What is the rarest M&M color?

Brown

77. What is the name of Jordan's capital city?

Amman

78. Which Roman Emperor liked to fight in games?

Commodus

79. Who discovered King Tut's tomb?

Howard Carter

80. Which country was the first to use paper currency?

China

81. Where was the U.S. largest surrender in battle?

Bataan

82. What is the family name of the ruling dynasty of Monaco?

Grimaldi

83. What grows from an acorn?

Oak Tree

84. When a people are frightened their ears produce more of what?

Earwax

85. In 1917 Finland declared its independence from which country?

Russia

86. Which continent is in all four hemispheres?

Africa

87. Who was said to float like a butterfly and sting like a bee??

Muhammed Ali

88. What is the world's most venomous fish?

Stonefish

89. What christian denomination was founded by John Wesley in 1738?

Methodist

90. The longest bridge in the world is located in which country

China

91. Who introduced the world's first mass-produced car?

Henry Ford

92. Which country was Joseph Stalin born in?

Georgia

93. What is the longest river?

Nile

94. In which U.S. state was the atomic bomb tested in?

New Mexico

95. How many US states begin with the letter A?

4

96. The southern tip of South America has what name?

Cape Horn

97. Who wrote Frankenstein?

Mary Shelley

98. Which of these instruments is used to measure wind speed?

Anemometer

99. How many U.S. Presidents were named James?

6

100. King Henry VI of England was also the king of which country?

France